BIRDS FLOCK FISH SCHOOL

Birds Flock
Fish School

Edward Carson

SIGNAL EDITIONS IS AN IMPRINT OF VÉHICULE PRESS

For Joyce

Published with the generous assistance of The Canada Council for the
Arts and the Canada Book Fund of the Department of Canadian Heritage.

SIGNAL EDITIONS EDITOR: CARMINE STARNINO

Cover design: David Drummond
Set in Filosofia and Minion by Simon Garamond
Printed by Marquis Book Printing Inc.

LIBRARY AND ARCHIVES CANADA CATALOGUING IN PUBLICATION

Carson, Edward, 1948-, author
Birds flock fish school / Edward Carson.

Poems.
ISBN 978-1-55065-359-5 (pbk.)

I. Title.

PS8555.A7724B57 2013   C811'.54   C2013-905906-7

Published by Véhicule Press, Montréal, Québec, Canada
www.vehiculepress.com

Distribution in Canada by LitDistCo
www.litdistco.ca

Distributed in the U.S. by Independent Publishers Group
www.ipgbook.com

Printed in Canada on FSC certified paper.

Things keep their secrets
HERACLITUS

Contents

ONE

The Language of Birds

1.

We're not sure how they
went missing: *only that they are*

Their soaring black wings once
were everywhere, appearing

and disappearing, splashing
past the stone bird bath.

But here, at the water's edge,
they are weightless now.

We seek out their loud calls
of merriment, so infectious.

We listen to the sudden rise
and fall of their swift feathers

fanning the water's edge,
invisible to the touch.

We search for them everywhere,
each one airless and waiting,

hovering in the fence as a blur
of yellow finches whistles by.

We are watchful for their precarious,
cautious balancing, how it quickly

wraps them, dark hooded
travelers all, in the water's shape.

We are watchful how they time
each fearful leap away, guarded

and full of the flight they find
will take them to the other side.

2.

Their breath is sinister and
invisible: *it leaves a mark unmistakable*

Inside the hesitant sky, the world
around them breathes in and out.

The dull clouds are not sure
what to make of these black sparks.

Their wings are a slipstream,
unseen, carried above whole oceans.

The pale blue mantle above them
rushes down to fan their flame.

Emerging from the glare
of a thousand thousand mornings

they swoop down upon us,
burrowing deep into our heads.

We are held in the crisp heyday
of their coming and going.

They are everything we fear
is ours, and cannot say no

to their coming. They are here
for a second, then gone.

Their hunger is everywhere.
We are unsure when they arrived,

when their iridescent, indelible
mark escaped in a blink of an eye.

So it is we cannot help but think
that something more is missing,

that the best we want to believe
in is what we cannot see,

that what we leave unsaid
is the voice inside that says too much.

3.

They are full of nameless
gardens: *nothing is more unattainable*

Except this morning their faint
swirl of wing and golden light

skims the garden's edge.
Like a spreading veil ready to blanket

everything it touches, this is a
herald of their new beginning

where nothing is so unattainable
as a mind set free, where

nothing is so futile as a mind
absorbing what it can no longer see.

We are unsure when they last
appeared. We are unsure of where

the sight of them might take us
next. We know them to be

uncomfortable in the unfamiliar
air, uneasy in their skins.

Around them a sharp stillness
is growing out of their marble eyes.

Something is moving them
into the sky, spreading their wings,

molding the invisible air
around them. How can we learn

more from what we cannot see
before us, but has always been there?

How can they all but disappear
into the ancient widening sky

with only their raucous calling
calling us to witness their vanishing?

Landscape

An immense precision is necessary, coming as it does,
amazed at the arrangement, between last light and field.

The land accumulates, always curving, apart from itself
as if everything depended on its arrival, as if its contents

were a cruel consequence, purposeful, crowding the sky.
No single pattern emerges, no sleight-of-hand topology,

undefined, escapes this field of gravity, this philosophy
of continuous time. All repercussions are immeasurable.

In this singularity, the human touch melts in acceleration,
an equation we maintain in history, in a future boldly

composed as if it were really going to happen, as if one
last array might bring us all to see what we least expect.

Daybreak

Begin full of mystery, joining of shade and light, the shape
of nothing in particular, at some point unformed, plainly

fluid, amorphous. Everything unites, at odds with itself,
opposite in flow, hard to combine, harder still to undo.

There is no thinking past its form, no scene less worthy
of the thought. The landscape, an extraction, emerges out

of itself, ambitious, embodying a frame that has no face.
No brutal fare cools the heart of this expression, no wise

illusion of the moment divides its rising points of light.
The occasion is geometric, the far horizon a mongrel line

rapidly moving away. All reason fades, all angles vanish,
the daybreak annealing this timely marriage of convenience.

Minutes

What vanishes, what is left behind, carelessly abandons
its continuous parts. Incidental as fresh rain drumming

on the roof, it measures you, mindfully crossing the room.
The pleasure is in watching, you say, in turning quickly

at a moment's notice, the hum of each new minute elusive
as honey bees. It would be impossible to believe in you

in any other time, unlikely and difficult to know what order
you bring to this aggregate of thinking, this elegant dance.

The invisible awaits us. Something about what has come
and gone swirls and eddies in our brains, hastily forgotten.

We must be patient, this blessing of the present absorbing
the past, releasing something different than understanding.

Rendezvous

Put into words, the nightfall finds itself translated, a meeting
of ripe perfumes, clouds awash, an attraction low in the west.

What are we to know of this? That there is only one clear way
into the night, its confession a confident dream in us, its canopy

a burning storyline of gods and goddesses? We see the horizon
lingers, speaking in tongues, slowly releasing the sky. Yet, hard

as it is to imagine, the night patiently awaits us, perfectly at ease,
safely celestial. It anticipates us at the head of the last remaining

light, a dark metaphor of itself. Then we will find sleep, dreaming
of rare fictions, unearthing a vital currency of stars falling loose

from the hybrid sky. In the end, will we find this to be what is here
for us to wonder, what dark embrace we covet, identical as heaven?

Presentation

Seamlessly arranged, adamantly punctual, now something
more than ordinary light, morning makes all the difference

in this slow, imperfect narrative, measuring itself against
all future tides. Its presentation is dense and timely, built

on current currents, targeted to weary, outstretched minds.
The morning speaks out and sets a path in the light and dark

fields of our belief. The morning sees that truth in telling
is not revealed in what it thinks or says, but finding itself

released like a stream from its knowing. Setting loose
the slow riddle of its voice, the morning shows the way

to what is meant to be, but harder still to say, what might
emerge from silence, overflowing, pushing the present on.

Crossroads

Familiar though these currents are, in favour of wishing
for more we measure out a new argument, a breezy talk

unraveling, fragrant as fact and fiction. The unwise between
us questions, buoyant in brain-heart, keeping all afloat all

night long through the dark, intimate and hard to believe in.
Our problem is in whether to remain unforeseen, or surface

snapping at what is necessary as air, intensive as breathing.
So calibrates the morning smile with the moon, the left hand

joined with the right. Every word in heaven and earth comes
to an unexpected head. Even without thinking, we now feel

everything, lacking for nothing, delicately pulling answers
out of hats, strangely confident in whatever happens along.

TWO

Codes

This incessant blinking, hooting, alphabet of prints
overcomes the mystery of its song, the secret lining

of its letters. It arrives continuously, calmly attentive
to details, tearing up its meaning, its spirit a desire

leaning in every direction possible. What is there
here to think about except our unease, the unsure

lost order and disorder of our craving, the longing
to know with certainty there is only one way back.

All issues are incidental, in time. At least from here
we see what resonates between us. A new opening

opens, a growing apparition in the shape of another,
beckoning, the sheer weight of seeing, the missing.

Signs

This confusion of one thing and its other, leaving
us full of wonder, knowing what isn't known.

And radiant too, so perfectly arranged, this patient
beauty of one thing blurred with its other, elusive

as last light—itself a blessing and a curse, pulling
together, orderly, ghost-like, ruthless in its timing.

A compelling tale, yearning to be heard, clarity urgently
escaping its design, baffling, yet clear in the telling.

One thing beckoning at the edges of another,
we think of things retrieved, our lives put together.

Until what signifies most is the argument of the two,
meeting, transforming, each in the play of response.

Riddles

This moment caught by an attentive gaze
full of cut glass edges, asides and pitfalls.

Continuous threads, a question and answer
of what turns against chance, order and flow.

This doubleness is luminous, always arriving
in the present, tense, bordering on language.

The illusion of complexity, elusive as mischief
releasing beams of light, brilliant mosaics of now.

Understood slowly, arriving well behind and late
in the day, obsessing over a mindless rhyme.

This is our fabric, full of auguries, what we know
ruptures the actual, the speech of noise and night.

Ciphers

This old mechanical order, blistering, thinking
through necessary attachments, observing the play

of algorithms, history, guessing at new outcomes.
The veils accumulate; undressed and transparent

we think in accretion of parts, meaning many
more things, emptying out of our breath, rattling

our undone, unknown pleasures. Measuring up
this key to a continuous stream, unlike any others,

of transition, reflecting to meaning, astonishing all.
Finding the missing, the vanishing, the sweet

vacancy is the last landscape we might expect to find
at the end of our search, at the edge of our skins.

Summoning

This progress of arrival, at first disordered and perplexing,
will not appear outside itself, so fine with line and fracture,

will not scorn return or find easy comfort, regret, in this its
slow emerging. Each entrance is a new foundation, a threshold

boldly curved and brightly bound, something wholly staged
for the large and common good, looking into, watching over,

stepping through each opening. Knowing little, we confess
to a complex collapse of night into day. This material light

is an old mystery, remote as conjuring, installing an invocation,
collimated, urgently infinite as the morning sun emptying itself.

In all of this the possibilities are endless, the birth of a paradigm
turned inside out, rehearsed and willing, stealing the only scene.

Puzzles

This bird in the snow, illusion of content, luminously
arriving late in the day, now staring into the cold,

now curving away, drawn to a background of detail.
What are we to solve in this? Are we to understand

what is seen or known, what fills the frantic eye
or empties the empty space, the bottomless sky?

This landscape caught emerging, the appearance
of meaning turned on its head, manifest realities

making mischief of our thinking. All of these are
ways of seeing the beginning of change, the other,

yet hardly noticing, looming up before us, elusive,
full of mysteries, constellations we can hardly bear.

Waiting

This slow unraveling, not thinking so its meaning
might surprise or find us wise beyond our years.

This life is more and less all guess and complicating
symmetries, not of this earth nor here in wisdom's eyes.

This might be what's going to be, like somewhere
brought up close to see, not soon upturned or turned

around, nor made to complicate or puzzle through
each beat of possibility. And what are we to think

of this, or even how we might have missed this wise
complexity? Not taken up before its time, now rising

slowly sign by sign, this place is what is known to be,
this loss of waiting, the last of all our vanishing.

Symptoms

This swelling that befell, altogether tender, vanished
unintended as an accident, returned, freshly chronic

in its progression, a mark of something largely more.
Not so much a nightmare, we think, or age's shadow,

this crossing of connected signs, indications of urgent
waves, dark vibrations descending, enveloping faith.

No mere abstraction now, here subjective to the core,
this slow accumulation gives patient measure to the risk.

The day breaks before we know it. Our restlessness
is impossible to subdue. A promise appears, invisible

as light, pushing past the literal, the loosely knit ideas
of what the only thing is on earth to know, to believe in.

THREE

Birds Flock Fish School

points a way forward, each new movement
moves them further along, shaping and circling

the group inside itself, wrapping the compact
cloud of their coming and going in a wave

of their own making. They move quickly to pass
along to each other a new thought, knowing

nothing of where each random turn will take
them. We sense a common spirit in this gathering

within ourselves, in this bold outline of another
world emerging. We are looking for a way inside

and out, looking to reclaim an old refrain of
escape, only to be found out where finding rests.

Undercurrents

We don't see what it is before us, but it will
surprise us in the way an unexpected current

can hold us in our place, can make us lean
fully into the hard muscle of its embrace.

The water pulling is pulling us into its arms,
inviting belief in the sheer power of its will.

We long to give ourselves over to its might,
to find in its flow something to find ourselves.

We understand its simple pleasures, pleasing
as it is to hear this simple, brief description

of our loving. In the diminishing light we see
in its steady pull what soon might come and go.

Fish School

Never more motionless as how we see them now,
where hardly a whisper gives them cause to move,

these fish are a white blur of meaning made more
real than we can know, their watery home a calm

they turn to in their wayward flight. The thought
of each is here for all to see, is here for all of us

to measure in the sharp evasions of their turning.
The curve of their unlikely path is what we wish

to know, is what we try to make of their going
and return. Their freedom from direction surprises us,

draws from us a longing for this journey to complete
itself before we come to the knowledge of its end.

Lost and Found

We watch for signs, but the signs aren't found.
At first, there are ragged shadows spilling over

the slow, white clouds, though at the start these
are only the birds, alone and airborne, calling.

But we take them at their word, seeing in their
gathering sway a growing dominance in the sky.

As the new moon turns the settling air to amber,
we think we might grasp how each of us who lose

our way will find ourselves again in the company
of what we cannot change. The birds are a map filling

our minds, calling us to see the shape of what
will go missing, of what we are destined to find.

Awakening

The shadow of the moon is enormous around us.
Someone asks a question, and then it's dawn.

Somewhere in the early hour the sky collapses
into itself. The energy it takes to fill this space

is well past the measure of gravity, brighter still
than the puzzle of heaven. The light is a blindness

we see waiting for us. We already understand
something has gone missing, and this revelation

arrives to block out the simplest of thoughts.
It happens every time we say something about

seeing what's coming for each of us, seeing
the sky fill with birds, overcoming the clouds.

Birds in the Water, Fish in the Sky

The icy water builds a reflection of you. Before
you move on, will you find no rest, no tranquil

appearance to answer the whirling winds, the absent
eye of flight? This winter sky is clear of all signs;

so brilliant blue, it has no resting point, is pulling
things forward to find in you a clue to another

form of complicity. Together this water and sky
are moving ahead, are part of a mind clearing itself

of what it knows it doesn't know, of what it thinks
will never rest, to find what's no longer there.

The Force that Keeps Things Afloat

1.

The water is clear as glass, flat and smooth,
a description of what the autumn leaf knows.

The force that keeps things afloat takes note
of what it is to be the falling leaf, imagines

the tension of its balancing, face up, against
the water pressing back. The water is more

than what the surface is, is less than the sky
above and the earth below. Looking at itself,

the surface finds a place for itself between
the water and air. And the falling leaf, tired

of what it knows to be at the centre of things,
finds a freedom in being exactly where it is.

2.

The force that keeps things afloat designs
a way of thinking around the winter's first

flurries of snow filtering through the air.
The snow falling finds the morning light

waiting, an intelligent patience filling the air.
Out of nothing, a growing optimism of white

takes the place of what is known to be there,
takes a pulse of what grows into questions

and answers connecting us to what might be.
The fresh snow cannot imagine more than

what it has become, cannot become more than
the silent surface of winter celebrating itself.

3.

A stiff wind begins before the end of spring,
carrying with it a nervous current of thought.

Made wary of thinking, the wind is curious
to say less and less, to think of a new way

around the surface of things. And so it skims
the day, barely acknowledging what escapes

its grasp. The force that keeps things afloat
is the wind thinking it knows better, reducing

the future to the unclear, living edge of things,
to the hollow silence of the birds not-calling,

to the muffled promise of a single voice, distant
singing, unsure of everything it has failed to say.

4.

This thinking we love leaves everything behind.
This thinking we feel in our heads is turning

itself around and into our hearts. This thinking
we love to find is fluid and wholly hard to lose.

It leaves us a memory the wide world thinks
as one thing, and knows as another. This thinking

is plural as snow, both buoyant and particular
as birds rising in a wind-filled sky. This thinking

is a force that keeps things afloat, understands
what a limitless thought that might be, leaving

us far behind. This thinking of what we love
most is everything we cannot begin to undo.

FOUR

Translation

At times, our reason flies beyond us, a final way of seeing
something lost in translation, an intimacy persuaded

into persistent thinking, a heart unraveled from inside out.
We prize the outcome of this philosophy, sample its ideas

at our pleasure. And pleasure it is, poised between a desire
to speak and the threshold of an overwhelming thought.

This is what the end of the day has come to, meditating
on *Meditations*, the horizon faltering, the setting sun a line

of true abstraction. Transitioning, the field's raw umber
elaborates before and after, the swarming blackbirds

hovering halfway between earth and sky. Everything
arrives on time. Something departs, ambitious, perfect.

Departing

Trajectories, low in the sky, the evening sun filtering
fields, wind spinning, calming, becoming a gradual

calculation in slow motion. Each beat of this allegiance
is interrupted, parenthetical, its incandescence pliable

as skin removing itself from all signs of all signs.
We cannot say how slow this vanishing, how quickly

gravity becomes us. Its measure makes a joy of passing.
Forgotten time, ignoring the mystery of the thinking heart,

remains a logic made real in the relief of a sudden loss.
We drift, following an orbit, undetected, misleading.

The present, being present, disperses here, this horizon
as deep as sleep, as deliberately silent as an undertow.

Prophesy

What will not set forth from the mind, comes to mind.
It presumes to know too little, then understands too much.

It defies belief, this singular thought, overpowering in its
conviction, a thunderous confrontation, rolling like a slow

intention of feeling, percussive, thumping hard against
our hearts. What overcomes us is a sound like no other.

What overwhelms is the certainty of thinking that lives
well past our last words together, that soon emerges in

the irresistible fabric of augury, foretold omens and signs.
We are forbidden to know what fails to remain, what returns

to us like a trajectory gone awry, until that closing moment
when the evening sky coruscates, the unknowable occurs.

Attenuation

Into this starry night, lives disperse, presently elusive,
or not present, continuously falling, flawlessly releasing

from an airy lens their pulsing repercussions, hiding
joys and sorrows, still. Fresh particles come and go,

haunting now this western sky, pointing to a meeting
place they're meant to be. What eludes our human hum

and beat, escapes its ever-present meaning, meaning
more than what's parting, less than it pretends to be.

What's passing, this wise subtraction from the whole
is looking less like loss or gain, ordered this way

in words, anew, focused in this starry night, a portrait
of arriving, colliding, fleeting, transparent as feeling.

Flying Formation

In the morning we come up carefully against
the clouds, not so much afraid of their height

as of the blindness they can bring. As far as
we can see, there's something to look into,

like the simple dread of travelling through
an emerging envelope of rain or fog or snow.

We come up against the clouds, their glowing
steep banks like light forgotten, craving itself.

Found so high above the revelations of the earth,
they describe what turns out to be the rising

shape of our fear, the abiding ghost of our falling,
the anxiety of what the world can offer next.

Watching Gravity

His falling is made static, looking up, now arching
for room against the symmetry of cloud and sky.

This burden of seeing, witnessing, what cannot be
averted, attaches a suffering constant as geometry.

New as the flow of currents, blindly invisible, its sum
provokes a turning away, ignoring an intervention

of belief. Spring has never been this clear, so stricken
in its meaning. It makes all our differences immense.

This restlessness, wholly quantified, becomes the pull
of knowing what lies outside ourselves, the story

that begins with an impossible picture of the world,
then moves away, having seen the incomprehensible.

Awaiting Radiance

Not puzzled by these passing times, nor rushing
past the missing signs of unrecollected lives,

not halfway there or half way back, nor even
near the nearest gap between this waking heart

and thought, not even knowing this or that, nor
thinking this is still a riddle slipping by, is still

a half-dream passing through that you and I
will soon undo, that you and I will soon undo.

We are this moment not unsure that what begins
begins to end before we even know its past, or

well before we know the moment of that end,
we know it's been a long time coming.

FIVE

Intensive Care

Releasing control, this complex of failing skin
is wheeled into a precarious balance, a room

with a purpose, humming lights reeling above,
gravity giving in. Here everything is measured,

hovering in anticipation of a navigation away
from how to think and feel. This is more than

the mystery of plunging into sleep, something
more than knowing what to do, how to arrive,

when to depart. Soon enough, time disappears
taking with it my head, arms, legs, the need

to understand, the capacity of mind, elsewhere,
slow to imagine your eyes, caring, unshakeable.

Portrait in a Room

The absence is in the place someone leaves
behind, departing the room without so much

as another word, an unlikely place to be thinking
someone might be searching for something else

entirely. It is the feeling left behind, this feeling
of a certain way of knowing what works best

and what might take its place. If there is a word
for it, it must be the boundary of what is no longer

there to see or know, the promise of a promise
not to be what we hoped or longed for, not to be

left alone in a room, but the promise of that final
hour when you spoke softly, slowly of everything.

Self-Portrait

What is not known informs this outline, delays the shape
of what is necessary, finds a relationship in the smallest

edge or curvature. The head regrets, swelling the day,
joined by long, eroded years, willing to be what should

not be, subtle as landscape. Yet the beating heart multiplies,
coming to see itself abundant, unfinished, full of unknown

mountains and appetite for stars. What is this likeness?
Self-contained, overwhelming in spirit, each similarity

releases another, vanishing into vanishing points, pointing
away from what is known. We would never think to query

what might be waiting, what remains in doubt, before what
shows before us moves, flourishing, closer to its passing.

Snow

1.

The snow falls and falls, looming before us
in the shape of a river, a bird, a tree, advancing

like a thought emerging from an empty space.
The snow falls and falls as the season's mind

comes into focus, is another motive for stillness,
is a clear, persistent climate emerging from above.

The snow falls and blankets our thinking. It falls
and searches for the knowledge of knowing

what to look for. The snow falls from a heaven
that gave it birth, falls until it has no other place

to go, no reason to arrive. The wisdom of falling
is in knowing where the sky will begin and end.

2.

Snow is a weather we covet now, falling head
first, dropping out of the cloud-filled sky. Snow

is the white map we carry forward in our minds,
a sign language expanding within the day. Snow

finds a path to our hearts, believes in the purity
and pull of gravity. Snow finds a way to know

the changing shape of winter, the eloquence of ice.
Snow becomes the voice we hear deep in the night,

filling in the names of the lost. In the emptying air,
snow is the cold hand of belief, the sharp eye of pride.

Snow becomes more than the wisdom of the fool,
the excess of the strong. It fills the shape of its falling.

First and Last Things

In the middle of a winter morning, a flock
of birds calls out as it carves through the sky.

When I breathe in next, waking, your thighs
straddling me, your white dress is billowing,

tenting us like blowing snow, and somehow
we are joined and rocking, joined and rocking.

I listen carefully to what you say. Your words
are miles ahead of my thinking, our timing off,

our directions different as currents coming up
against each other. What we think of as buoyancy

is nothing like seduction, a revelation building
like an craving. Beyond our thinking, nothing lasts.

Acknowledgements

My thanks to the good people at Vehicule Press for all their hard work, planning and execution. In particular, the work of my editor, Carmine Starnino, was truly exceptional and exactly what the manuscript needed. He dared for a lot, and his judgments were spot on.

Special thanks also go out to Brian for his support, insightful readings and reactions to this work.

Finally, I acknowledge with special pleasure the work of the Poem, which continues to allow me into its inner workings. I know it knows something I don't know, so that writing each and every poem allows me yet another chance at uncovering the centre of something so much larger than us all.

Signal
EDITIONS

Carmine Starnino, Editor
Michael Harris, Founding Editor

SELECTED POEMS David Solway
THE MULBERRY MEN David Solway
A SLOW LIGHT Ross Leckie
NIGHT LETTERS Bill Furey
COMPLICITY Susan Glickman
A NUN'S DIARY Ann Diamond
CAVALIER IN A ROUNDHEAD SCHOOL Errol MacDonald
VEILED COUNTRIES/LIVES Marie-Claire Blais (Translated by Michael Harris)
BLIND PAINTING Robert Melançon (Translated by Philip Stratford)
SMALL HORSES & INTIMATE BEASTS Michel Garneau
    (Translated by Robert McGee)
IN TRANSIT Michael Harris
THE FABULOUS DISGUISE OF OURSELVES Jan Conn
ASHBOURN John Reibetanz
THE POWER TO MOVE Susan Glickman
MAGELLAN'S CLOUDS Robert Allen
MODERN MARRIAGE David Solway
K. IN LOVE Don Coles
THE INVISIBLE MOON Carla Hartsfield
ALONG THE ROAD FROM EDEN George Ellenbogen
DUNINO Stephen Scobie
KINETIC MUSTACHE Arthur Clark
RUE SAINTE FAMILLE Charlotte Hussey
HENRY MOORE'S SHEEP Susan Glickman
SOUTH OF THE TUDO BEM CAFÉ Jan Conn
THE INVENTION OF HONEY Ricardo Sternberg
EVENINGS AT LOOSE ENDS Gérald Godin (Translated by Judith Cowan)
THE PROVING GROUNDS Rhea Tregebov
LITTLE BIRD Don Coles
HOMETOWN Laura Lush
FORTRESS OF CHAIRS Elisabeth Harvor
NEW & SELECTED POEMS Michael Harris
BEDROCK David Solway
TERRORIST LETTERS Ann Diamond
THE SIGNAL ANTHOLOGY Edited by Michael Harris
MURMUR OF THE STARS: SELECTED SHORTER POEMS Peter Dale Scott
WHAT DANTE DID WITH LOSS Jan Conn
MORNING WATCH John Reibetanz
JOY IS NOT MY PROFESSION Muhammad al-Maghut
    (Translated by John Asfour and Alison Burch)
WRESTLING WITH ANGELS: SELECTED POEMS Doug Beardsley
HIDE & SEEK Susan Glickman
MAPPING THE CHAOS Rhea Tregebov
FIRE NEVER SLEEPS Carla Hartsfield
THE RHINO GATE POEMS George Ellenbogen
SHADOW CABINET Richard Sanger
MAP OF DREAMS Ricardo Sternberg
THE NEW WORLD Carmine Starnino
THE LONG COLD GREEN EVENINGS OF SPRING Elisabeth Harvor

KEEP IT ALL Yves Boisvert (Translated by Judith Cowan)
THE GREEN ALEMBIC Louise Fabiani
THE ISLAND IN WINTER Terence Young
A TINKERS' PICNIC Peter Richardson
SARACEN ISLAND: THE POEMS OF ANDREAS KARAVIS David Solway
BEAUTIES ON MAD RIVER: SELECTED AND NEW POEMS Jan Conn
WIND AND ROOT Brent MacLaine
HISTORIES Andrew Steinmetz
ARABY Eric Ormsby
WORDS THAT WALK IN THE NIGHT Pierre Morency
    (Translated by Lissa Cowan and René Brisebois)
A PICNIC ON ICE: SELECTED POEMS Matthew Sweeney
HELIX: NEW AND SELECTED POEMS John Steffler
HERESIES: THE COMPLETE POEMS OF ANNE WILKINSON, 1924-1961
    Edited by Dean Irvine
CALLING HOME Richard Sanger
FIELDER'S CHOICE Elise Partridge
MERRYBEGOT Mary Dalton
MOUNTAIN TEA Peter Van Toorn
AN ABC OF BELLY WORK Peter Richardson
RUNNING IN PROSPECT CEMETERY Susan Glickman
MIRABEL Pierre Nepveu (Translated by Judith Cowan)
POSTSCRIPT Geoffrey Cook
STANDING WAVE Robert Allen
THERE, THERE Patrick Warner
HOW WE ALL SWIFTLY: THE FIRST SIX BOOKS Don Coles
THE NEW CANON: AN ANTHOLOGY OF CANADIAN POETRY
    Edited by Carmine Starnino
OUT TO DRY IN CAPE BRETON Anita Lahey
RED LEDGER Mary Dalton
REACHING FOR CLEAR David Solway
OX Christopher Patton
THE MECHANICAL BIRD Asa Boxer
SYMPATHY FOR THE COURIERS Peter Richardson
MORNING GOTHIC: NEW AND SELECTED POEMS George Ellenbogen
36 CORNELIAN AVENUE Christopher Wiseman
THE EMPIRE'S MISSING LINKS Walid Bitar
PENNY DREADFUL Shannon Stewart
THE STREAM EXPOSED WITH ALL ITS STONES D.G. Jones
PURE PRODUCT Jason Guriel
ANIMALS OF MY OWN KIND Harry Thurston
BOXING THE COMPASS Richard Greene
CIRCUS Michael Harris
THE CROW'S VOW Susan Briscoe
WHERE WE MIGHT HAVE BEEN Don Coles
MERIDIAN LINE Paul Bélanger (Translated by Judith Cowan)
SKULLDUGGERY Asa Boxer
SPINNING SIDE KICK Anita Lahey
THE ID KID Linda Besner
GIFT HORSE Mark Callanan
SUMPTUARY LAWS Nyla Matuk
THE GOLDEN BOOK OF BOVINITIES Robert Moore
MAJOR VERBS Pierre Nepveu (Translated by Donald Winkler)
ALL SOULS' Rhea Tregebov
THE SMOOTH YARROW Susan Glickman
THE GREY TOTE Deena Kara Shaffer
HOOKING Mary Dalton
DANTE'S HOUSE Richard Greene
BIRDS FLOCK FISH SCHOOL Edward Carson